where the
memory was

Hibaq Osman

JACARANDA

TWENTY
in 2020
Black Writers, British Voices

This edition first published in Great Britain 2020
Jacaranda Books Art Music Ltd
27 Old Gloucester Street,
London WC1N 3AX
www.jacarandabooksartmusic.co.uk

A CIP catalogue record for this book is available from the British
Library

ISBN: 9781913090142
eISBN: 9781913090340

Cover Image: Christina Schweighardt
Jacket Design: Rodney Dive
Typeset by: Kamillah Brandes

Printed and bound by CPI Group (UK) Ltd, Croydon, CR0 4YY

بِسْمِ اللهِ الرَّحْمٰنِ الرَّحِيْمِ

For those searching

Contents

Part One

Part Two

Part Three

Part One

*All that came before me
knows me better than I know myself*

Packing Two Gold Necklaces

When there is talk of warriors
rarely do they mention the keepers of secrets
or how whole cities have been moved
under the cloak of night
what tiresome work it is
to carry lineage

which is to hold
your great grandmother and great grandchild
in one hand
and a tasbeeh in the other
you say inshaAllah, God will free us
and prepare for the unknown

often, water

often, death

When there is talk of warriors
the bustle of kitchens is omitted,
but recipes are strategically altered
in new weather
on new lands
isn't a sword just a knife
that has been repurposed?

Which proves you have made do
behind the curtains of sons
and into the long memories of your daughters
whose minds are a maze of language
that cannot translate your name

Nobody will speak of what you left behind
to carry us forward,
least of all yourself
instead:

Allahu aclam /

God knows best

2010

you have carefully curved your torso into an almost s
reaching over for the garlic, mind the heartbreak
don't spill the wars, we sit
shoulders sinking into the wooden gap of a dinner chair
and wonder what part of the tree accepts our fat?
must be the soul, we decide

the splinters between us have been named

2003

you are cutting the back of
your hair without a mirror
the new husband chews, stinks up the house
i nod / too much tea
i nod / he's not even tall
we laugh, neither is dad
your small men and their merry misfortune
i vow never to repeat a mistake
tell you it looks fine
short hair suits you
but you cut until you see scalp
"there" you say
"now i can go"

Failed DNA Test

tells me i am mainly made up of the things i like about you least
such as my tendency to leave only the ghost of myself
in strange corners, waiting

when they split me open
a smaller version of yourself might appear where my courage should be
would i recognise the newborn as mine?

or expect another type of phantom much like you did?

A Brief History

We scheduled our family holidays around court dates. Never
took the same route home. Some things were only to be
spoken about in the house, with the door locked after the
school run. Kids are fast but rumours are faster.
Serenity was what we borrowed from neighbours in half-cup
weight. Shared anything but the shame. What is ours is yours
but don't ask about our son, or our daughter, or the children
before that. Mohammed was splashed with acid and moved north.
Our family has a habit of doing that, moving until the past stops
chasing. I haven't seen him since the news. Scandal in the
blood and scandal in the soil. Spilling out of everything that is
created with this name.

Family Tree Full of Parentheses

perhaps this torment was handmade for you
so vast that you cannot outrun the stories of your blood
be wary of the devil you know, how it can erupt loneliness
and the curse of ancestry. the tale mothers whisper
to their daughters as they braid duaa into their scalps.
it is a conflict you know too well. we come from a long line
of liars and shepherds, take your pick. perhaps you will become
a student of empathy or a rescuer, take your pick. they say
in every marriage there is both

Hospital Bands as Signet Rings

This ward is a tomb

       holding secrets of ritual, alongside our bodies

It is a pre-written will

       signed by the heads of the household

The morticians did their best work

       cutting the curse out where they could

Tumours outlive surgical knives

       and the cells that created them

This family is a tomb

       holding our bodies, alongside secrets of ritual

We are heads of the household

       turned morticians, turned writers of deeds

Trying to outlive our tumours

       and the cells that created them

on the hands of the saved, there will be no stains

we are born of what we bear and the charm that follows
ayeeyo fadumo has repented
for children she may never meet
we're sure she has kept us here
following the starlight, to say ameen and kiss her soles
darkness as henna has made itself
home in the gaps between her fingers

what scars could last here?

what history would be worthy?

we are born of charm and we bear what follows
there is a suitcase with both your names on it
carried like shield wherever you moved, or stayed
soil from every city and an etching from each lover
ayeeyo fadumo has repented for children she may never meet
a newborn hidden in the petals of her palm
we say ameen, and kiss her soles

When It Began

your child tells you
they do not like where they are

there are so many signs you have missed

later, fingers on beads you overhear them telling God
they were born from the flick of a fist

that this must be the darkness finally catching up

years later, bold and bloody they ask

'weren't you lonely, too
when you found out your body was not yours?'

Prototype

Black lullaby
the body is just a sample
on top of a sample,
on top of a sample

For example the body
is just a Black lullaby
on top of a sample,
on top of a sample

Part Two

I have remembered mine
remembered myself
remembered me
into tomorrow

the self help aisle is a scam

you, island of apprehension
attic with no ladder
have poured yourself into work

mimicking the smiles your aunties wear
this week you try rice milk
do not ask about the mechanics

would bathe in it if you could
rinse your eyeballs out
apologise for the bodies they've seen

try to outrun the sugar in your blood
like you did the men
and the boys before that

in front of the mirror you stand and
ask: who was the last person to visit
and not take?

tomorrow, you will free yourself
but now you pray for peace or
malak al-mawt

Three Week Log

Rest itself has become a chore
your body is now a ghost's whisper
something that could easily have been
a hallucination, nightmare with bones
you question its tangibility

you've thought long about
what friendship could do to you when you
feel you do not even exist

you've forgotten the proper way to
shake hands - two kisses
on each cheek
or one?

You count how many people you thanked
for their time, for their smiles
you sleep still counting

The tiles you stare at wear from the centre out
a spider-web crack,
it feels like looking in a mirror

An Exercise in Stopping Breath

When you meet for dinner,
he hugs your waist and you recoil
What used to be chemistry is now
the slow fusing of your skin to his.

How does one explain the body
yearning to leave before the heart does?
You slow eat a plate of goodbye
When the breakup comes, you'll be grateful

and he'll be heartbroken.
People will blame him when they find your corpse
two weeks pass without having shared with your friends

لَا يُكَلِّفُ اللَّهُ نَفْسًا إِلَّا وُسْعَهَا

You google the duration of a silent scream, when you
bleed out you don't want it to be messy.
The river by your estate is the clearest
reflection you've seen in months,
it is as ugly and necessary as you are. Somewhere,
an astrologer and an imam laugh heartily.

When you return to your house/coffin
your living room can say: here is a plant
she watered, she was very good at caring
for things other than herself.
New tenants will know you left peacefully. Your family
will know the hallucinations are over.

A Brief History II

In many ways my brothers and sisters are not my brothers
and sisters. That's how documentation goes. Take what you
can get and it'll save you in the long run. Or at least until the
resilience is battered out of you. I think these blocks were made
of the same clay my mother is made of. Tall and strong but never
warm. We've passed the oldest daughter curse back and forth
between us. A no match transfusion that will surely kill one
before the other. I pray it's me. In this house that is not a home,
we have four walls made of grief and a ceiling made of disappear-
ances that were never explained. Like adero's limbs that suddenly
vanished as if they decided his body, or this land, could not
contain them.

spatial awareness

there is a place for special girls
sometimes it's the house next door,
the aunts, or the youth centre
where they first learn what recoil is

here, the first lips to touch skin
will not be those they dreamt about
plush and young with passion
they may not feel like lips at all

where they slowly learn what time is
and isn't. how fragile the seconds
are when you count in silence
how the stopping, doesn't stop

sometimes this special place
holds unrelated remembrances
and suddenly you are crying at
a picture of a funny hat from that party

there have been so many parties

praying hands and prying eyes
the tv box becomes saviour
you have memorised whole films
this way, static on eyelids

match the tempo of blood rush
if this character, and that character
were locked in a room
where would the air go?

girls like us, bed frames no
mattresses. one pillow too much
not a restful night between
always falling off somewhere
or falling into ourselves

Sharp Objects Not Permitted

There is a specific history of secret diaries
woven into the undergarments of blush faced women
held under elastic and law

Once admitted
the nurses remind you of what you can carry
in your hands, under your tongue

You being who you are
fight the impulse to take this as a challenge

An Oyster Card as Citizenship

This city spills out
of our nails at this job,
or that job, we say everything twice
loosening our tongues each time
which speech pattern will we
tie ourselves to once we leave?

A fence to the side of our homes collapses
and stays like that for 3 years
two kids were injured
haven't seen them play out since

Moving because the memories leave wounds
A season passes and we are still outside

Praise and pay come in the form
of our bodies falling apart, weigh
the empty oyster again and again
we are young enough not to care
for a little while longer

Snapshots of Nightmares

The knock on your door   is a debt collector or your
conscience warning you sometimes death visits and expects
payment   uncertain of how he got in you could have been
a better host

When you run from home you'll pass this street exactly 82 times
the trees here never sing   midnight crows posed as friends peer
into the black of your pupils begging   you to greet them back

Always been a little slow to love and to unlocking doors us working
class kids   with volcanoes in our guts   we are time travellers
with more chances than we believe

93-94

In these circles around a shared meal
we weave our similarities into the tablecloth
reach for hands that will never abandon us
and rest on shoulders
memory foamed to the size of our cheeks
we can't speak for laughter
hysteric mouths wide with belonging

We spend whole evenings like this
no care for last orders or where we'll sleep
we'd lay here if we could
arms crocheted
each of us holding exactly the other two
with no space for air

It's not the Answer or the Question

wanting it to work and forcing it to work
are two different things
this room is too small, i can't get lost in it
i do not offer up my thoughts
hide them under the mattress, too
when he asks, i say nothing
suicide is a passing comment
that scares those around me

to turn a hand on shoulder
into a neck grip
takes all but a twist of the forearm
i know this too well
when he is done i walk quietly

time slowing at the start of my spine
sometimes, a graveyard feels like home
swollen with flesh but ultimately
decaying, i have been told

that wanting it to work and forcing it to work
are two different things
so i take another deep breath
and start acting like i'm listening

Malfunction at Turnham Green

You have mastered the art of getting by. World-renowned pretender. Birds keep knocking their beaks on your windows. Sometimes you think of yourself as one of them but lack courage. How confidently they run to their deaths. This is the second time this week you can't handle the sunlight, or your reflection. Outside there is a memorial for the deadlines you have missed. You've got a twitch in your left eyebrow that the hypnotist says is a breakdown waiting to happen. You eagerly ask how much longer? Tell her you do not have enough limbs to wait. You have been in need of servicing for years now. This is the first time anyone has noticed. Will they hold a parade for you? Tell me which flowers you'd choose, I'm sure we can arrange something. Would your family come to mourn if you left them to see your brother? Would you take him flowers too? They would not give you a muslim funeral but we can always hope. Maybe hope is in abundance on the other side. Maybe you would not have to pretend so hard.

Mantra for Restless Nights and Restless Beginnings

Consider yourself safe here
between pillows stuffed with chance
a parakeet on your window whistling into the breeze
there will be a night long enough for you to sink in
dreams you can dance into
and breakfast in the morning
all this is to come all this is to come all this to come

Part Three

If these memories created us,
shouldn't we dance in them?

say it again so we don't forget

i am sceptical of anything that moves inside of me
like your hand, curled at the tip of your fingers
you are long limbed heavy across my torso

angel-faced peril / while you sleep i trace
the wounds of grieving wings

i have waited years for a kiss to be home-coming
wanting something so vast and filling

with our masks on, we look brighter than ever
in my dreams i have disappeared with you

or stayed. been present longer than i knew possible
today is another something-i-can't-name

i am not running out of time
swallowing water from the depths of you

if nothing else, let's crack our bones together
in this small city where the sun sets red on our backs

we'll return to showers in london
a drop of rain for every reason we were kept apart

but today, let's find out
how hard we could love / where nobody knows our names
or what we owe each other

i didn't plan to stay long

love me in the sunbeams or not at all is all that i ask
the sides of my face i am most scared of
where the past no longer shades
a future i never envisioned
maybe you are the train wreck i've been running to
i have one-track-minded you to tomorrows
how tangled is tangled, really? this time,
one arm across another
glass blowers shaping an endless cup
this metal workmanship, this welding
we have forged new beginnings in the dregs

Things We Held Up Against Each Other

When the lights cut and
all that is left is a thought
I have of love

as cosmic entity,
a sound wave that loops always
before this,

I considered peeling skin to its last thick layers
but what then, is left to claim?

I have thought of love
after this as tectonic plates,
a crack that starts at knuckle
and finds itself trespassing on vertebrae

sending shivers down to cuticles

I have thought of love how it stands today,
as sweet side of tongue,
the sharpness of your "yes"
aching its way through silences repeating:
maybe, someday

A Brief History III

Was it the schizophrenia? Was it the schizophrenia?
Was it the schizophrenia? Is it coming for me next?
My grandma told me I look like her. Big in the same
ways but too quiet, she says. Like my mother, she
says, too many secrets in my eyes. I held her hands
as if the peace in her palms could free me. While she asks
what took me so long to visit. Why I'm not staying.
If I have to choose between my father's name and my mother's,
I choose calamity. I choose the sickness that will surely follow.
I choose recognising what cannot be healed. Like this house,
this mind and these names. I choose staying anyway.

Six Days

let's pretend we've been cast in a Wong Kar-Wai film
my favourite name is the rolling of letters off your tongue

when you tell me you miss me
and the longing eats away at our minds

there is a new lonely
in wanting someone you cannot have yet
we have waited, eager
to accept promises neither of us can fulfil

tell me it has always been me
the "yes" you quiver for
that nobody else's lips
feel quite as good

tell me this is all we'll ever want
even on our colourless days

We Sounds Better Than You or Me

I've been warned not to walk too much in areas where the lights dim to nothing and bodies end up in canals. You tell me to be safe, don't lurk. I take comfort in knowing that an estate is an estate, is an estate.

The next morning I tell you raspberry is my favourite flavour dessert and you say that doesn't count. I count it. Isn't everything better with a little bitter first? You disagree.

"What's the point of dessert then if all you take from it is pain?"
"Can't you just let anything be good?"

This is good, I say.

Or I could catch an uber. I could engage with a stranger who will always ask me if I'm dating or married or if perhaps I am too young. Baby face for a babygirl, one will say. I do not recount these stories to you, who will tell me "next time, don't get an uber - let me call you a proper cab" as if the white men are any different. To get to you, I could always catch an uber.

You peel the fruit slices off your upside down cake. Set them by the teabag. I mumble that my next poem will be about you and you better not die before I finish it. If time could hold us hostage I'd ask for it to keep us there.

You question why it has to be death or nothing.

"I don't mind how you get here just come"

I'll title it raspberry.

44

Cravings

i said i love you like a sigh
full of regretful hope

full of 'can't you see me here
dying to love you'

this world too small
these words too short

an encyclopaedia of loving you
falls from my lips

into a hole in my torso
where i swear to never release it

               really i love you like a vulture
    taking entire chunks of you into my mouth

        and padding my throat with your flesh
                  until you say enough

  you have had your fill, leave some for tomorrow
           but future is not currency here

      i have no stakes in what may come
    i say i love you like "please. a little more"

  as if i can not hear your pulse between my teeth

In The End There Was Only This

(after Ma$e's – Feel So Good)

The way I met you

curveball to chance, nemesis of fate
or proof of it
caught light in the corridor of early adulthood
stranger things are happening
and sharing a bed never felt so easy

Love rewinds itself until we trip on sacred shame
we are fistfight foundations,
the clarity after a bruise heals

this static is as much in my veins as it is yours
doom or destiny, curse or a blessing
these candle-wax memories
that I have let burn in my palms

The way you met me

young heart broke too easy
whole lot of stories in these CDs
we tempted the heavens with our laughter
chased bodies through dusk
I guess we're still running

Love celebrates the faults in us
The broken rings loud until we
sanitise our sins and start again

"Maybe this time" we sigh
but know a hack-job affair is all we were promised

Still, we're an adlib that plays out when the singing is done
our love a fading instrumental
After all this time
still wouldn't change you if I could

dreaming in parables

the mountains between us now a
new white sheet
you were a mirage / last slow burn of sun
on the days losing is all we've got
i have emptied my heart beneath your laughter
thought of open plains
and the regrowth we are chasing

don't spare me
love
don't spare my
love

ignore the age creeping around our eyes
swear i could feel your smile from cities over
when you say you love me,
what does that look like?
find your limit / like i find mine
every sip of you
a testament to my strength

Triage

I am never seen by the doctor
with the kind eyes though she tells me
"just a moment sweetheart"

There is an emergency centre in your
ribcage late nights I have rested here
amongst the bustle of the screening rooms

I think she is your mother
you have the same smile
she cares for me like you

a planet orbiting the sun
just enough space
for the light to pass through

And in Health

There are crows at this wedding
wings enveloping the bouquets
they too are
questioning the validity of lifelong love
of hands always being held
of a ship being swayed by two winds
before feasting
on leftover cake

Acknowledgements

First and foremost without the guidance of my family I would never have taken a chance on any of my writing. To my mother - thank you for reminding me I have been doing this longer than I have been doing most things, and that I can. To my baby sister Radwa who I always default to when I need to hear a thought out loud, and my brothers Yusuf and Zakaria who have given me pause when needed: your support and laughter are the two things that have made this possible. Thank you to my older sister Samiya, as well as my nephews and nieces, Sam you're the greatest mother ever. I'm thankful for my dearest aunt Laki, as well as Ahmed and Zahra for being supportive and continuing to hype me up all these years. I love you all.

I'd like to thank my friends, many of who inspired these poems and whose friendship has given me the strength to make it through writing and editing this. I am forever learning from and leaning on you. Thank you to: Keniyah, Sharmake, Reem, Nathan, Ayan, Huda, Naomi, Herb, Maryam, Torry, Greg, Hibaq, JJ, Mohammed, Naima, Hiba, Kamar, Charlene, Mariam, Eugenia, Sagal, Malcolm, Maria, Amran and Emilio! The love you have shared with me is the driving force behind everything I do; I hope you all know that. A loving thanks to friends and fellow writers who have held my hand through this and so much more: Rachel Long, Sumia Jaama, Bayan Goudarzpour, Amina Jama, Omar Bynon, Kareem Parkins-Brown, Amaal Said, Belinda Zhawi, Antosh Wojcik, Victoria Bulley, Sean Mahoney, Ruth Sutoyé, Tobi Kyeremateng. A special thank you to the entire OCTAVIA POETRY COLLECTIVE and many other groups and spaces I've been a part of. I could write pages and pages for each of you.

Thank you to Mr. Holloway for telling me this day would come.

Thank you to Jacaranda for giving me an opportunity to share my work, for being an independent publisher who prioritised our voices and invited me to be a part of a beautiful campaign. In particular I'd like to thank Magdalene Abraha who is an absolute storm to work with, who treated me with care and joy and never let a question go unanswered. Thank you to Nick Makoha for his editing eye and to Kamillah Brandes for guiding me through the production process. I'd also like to thank the rest of the Jacaranda team and congratulate the entire #Twentyin2020 cohort of writers. It's been amazing working alongside you!

To everybody who has ever read my work, came out to a reading, bought or downloaded anything I've put out before this point. Thank you, thank you, and thank you! I hope you like these poems. I am always rooting for you.

Hibaq

About the Author

Hibaq Osman is a Somali writer and reader raised in West London. According to her primary school teachers there are two things she has never stopped doing: talking and writing poems. Pushed by a brilliant community of family and friends, Hibaq first started sharing her work at open mic events which lead to headlining across the country, winning slams, joining collectives and judging prizes.

Her debut poetry pamphlet 'A Silence You Can Carry' was published with Out-Spoken Press in 2015 while she completed her degree in Psychology and Counselling. Since this publication, Hibaq has self-published two online pamphlets: 'the heart is a smashed bulb' (2017) and CARVINGS (2019) as well as graduating with a masters in Psychiatric Anthropology. Though her interests may seem unrelated, Hibaq's ideal world is one that includes art and expression at the forefront of healing and community care.

As a member of OCTAVIA POETRY COLLECTIVE, Hibaq Osman works towards a future where funding and access to the arts for all is the norm and not an exception. You can often find Hibaq in any free public space, using her precious writing time to tweet about R&B instead.